P9-BYO-254

CHILDREN SAVE
THE
RAIN FOREST

Dorothy Hinshaw Patent

PHOTOGRAPHS BY

Dan L. Perlman

COBBLEHILL BOOKS/DUTTON

New York

*To the children of the world
and especially to our own—
David, Jason, and Jeremy.*

ACKNOWLEDGMENTS

The author and photographer wish to give thanks to Ree Sheck, Omar Coto, and John Boll, who generously gave us time from their busy lives, and to the community at San Gerardo. We also want to thank the Forest Guards: Gerardo Sespedes Rodriguez, Ervedy Sanchez Zamara, Miguel Angel Salazar Castro, who helped Dan Perlman on his trip to the Poco Sol region of the Children's Rain Forest. Thanks, too, to Roland Smith, who came up with the idea and helped us team up, and to Nora and Greg for their support as we created this book.

Library of Congress Cataloging-in-Publication Data

Patent, Dorothy Hinshaw.
    Children save the rain forest / Dorothy Hinshaw Patent ;
photographs by Dan L. Perlman.
       p.   cm.
    Includes index.
    Summary: Explores the International Children's Rain Forest, what
it is, the plants and animals that live there, why it is important,
and what can be done to preserve it.
    ISBN 0–525–65163–2
    1. Rain forests—Juvenile literature. 2. Rain forest
conservation—Costa Rica—Juvenile literature. 3. Bosque Eterno de
los Niños (Costa Rica)—Juvenile literature.   [1. International
Children's Rain Forest (Costa Rica) 2. Rain forest conservation—
Costa Rica. 3. Rain forests. 4. Conservation of natural
resources.]   I. Perlman, Dan L., ill.   II. Title.
    QH86.P38   1996
    574.5'2642'0913—dc20   95–24533   CIP   AC

Published in the United States by Cobblehill Books, an affiliate of Dutton Children's Books,
a division of Penguin USA Inc., 375 Hudson Street, New York, New York 10014

Designed by Charlotte Staub
Printed in Hong Kong   First Edition
10 9 8 7 6 5 4 3 2 1

CONTENTS

The trunks of many rain forest trees are covered with other plants.

CHAPTER ONE

ENCOUNTERING THE RAIN FOREST

Ⓖ〜〜〜〜Ⓞ

I barely avoid falling as my boot catches on a tough root crossing the rugged trail that winds through the Central American rain forest. I'm with a college group hiking to San Gerardo, Costa Rica, a tiny outpost about three miles from the nearest passable road. The rest of the group is far enough ahead of me that I can pretend that I'm the only human exploring this gorgeous green realm.

Here and there, tiny delicate flowers litter the path. I look up, expecting to see blossoms. There are none in sight. My eyes follow the trunks of giant trees stretching toward the distant sun, and I see how the trees spread their branches at their tops, filling the spaces between them with a dense mantle of leaves. The treetops block out so much of the sunlight that I feel as if I'm wearing dark glasses. I wonder about the flowers lying on the trail. They are quite fresh—where did they come from?

I notice an amazing variety of plants clinging to the tree trunks and living nestled in the hollows where branches join the trunks. How can these plants survive, perched high in the air, so far from the ground in which more familiar plants are always rooted? Broad-leaved vines wind up the trunks from the forest floor toward the sunlight, while strands of roots and vines hang down toward the ground from far above. Tarzan would feel at home here.

Evidence of abundant animal life surrounds me—chewed edges of leaves drooping from a trailside plant, columns of ants racing up and down tree trunks. Now

1

Rain forest insects, such as this walking stick, are always feeding on leaves.

The trunks of some plants in the forest bear sharp spines.

and then, the grunting hoots of howler monkeys fill the forest. Delicate orange and black butterflies flit across the path. I hear the sweet songs of many birds, mixed with the strange metallic "bonk" of the three-wattled bellbird. I look all around for the birds, but they are nowhere in view—why can't I see them?

The temperature is cool, but my skin is damp. The moisture-filled air feels heavy. My left foot almost slips out from under me on the muddy trail, but I catch myself with my walking stick. I think of the warning we were given—if you start to fall, don't reach out to grab a support. Inch-long ants with vicious stings might be found here. They could be climbing about on any branch or tree trunk. Better to fall in the mud than get stung by one of these aggressive creatures. Besides, the trunks of many palms and ferns bear sharp spines that could easily pierce my hand.

I see light ahead as the trail turns and rises. I walk faster, and in a minute I'm out of the forest, squinting at the sudden sunlight. Before me lies a bright green meadow ringed by enormous craggy trees. Beyond the meadow are rugged forested hills, framing the view of a distant lake next to a cloud-topped volcano. From this vantage point I can see that the crowns of some trees are cloaked in blossoms—white for one, pink for another, and yellow for still a different one. No wonder I couldn't find the source of the flowers littering the trail—they grew drenched in light atop the forest giants.

Graceful black and white birds with long, forked tails circle effortlessly over the forest and the clearing. As I take in the scene, my eyes spot movement and a flash of brilliant color to my right—a huge iridescent blue *Morpho* butterfly flits by along

The clearing at San Gerardo.

3

Swallow-tailed kite in flight.

When this Morpho butterfly takes wing, the iridescent blue on the tops of the wings flashes in the sunlight.

the edge of the trees. So many birds are singing from high in the trees and along the edges of the forest that I can't tell where one song ends and another begins.

I stand in one place and soak up the beauty. I feel a wave of joy, followed by gratitude to the children of the world, who have saved this place. I'm in the Bosque Eterno de los Niños (Children's Eternal Forest), known in English as the International Children's Rain Forest. Thanks to money sent by children from around the world, more than 40,000 acres of Costa Rican forest have been saved from destruction, including this magical spot at San Gerardo.

My brief encounter with the forest makes me eager to learn about this special environment, about why the rain forest is so full of life, and to share that knowledge with others.

Rain Forest Symbol—The Keel-Billed Toucan

The colorful keel-billed toucan has become a familiar symbol of the rain forest. This appealing bird lives from the Mexican tropics southward through Central America into northern Colombia and northwestern Venezuela and from sea level up to 4,500 feet (1,300 meters). Its blackish body is decorated by a red patch under the tail and a red-edged bright yellow bib that reaches up to cover its face. The area around the eye is pale green, and its legs are bright blue. But the toucan's most striking feature is its giant, rainbow-colored bill. Its bill looks very heavy, but is actually hollow and lightweight. An adult male keel-billed toucan, which measures about 18½ inches (47 centimeters) long including the bill, weighs only a little over a pound (500 grams).

The toucan bill may be light in weight, but it is a useful tool for plucking fruit from the tips of branches. Toucans are mainly fruit eaters, but also feed on insects, small lizards, and snakes, if the opportunity arises. Grabbing food may be easy for the toucan, but swallowing is another matter. In order to swallow, a toucan must toss its head up and back, throwing the food from the tip of the bill into the throat.

Toucans group together in small, loose flocks of up to six birds. Besides living in the rain forest, toucans may venture into trees at the edge of the forest along rivers or pastures. There, they may call to one another, making a sound like a chorus of big frogs.

Keel-billed toucans nest in large cavities in trees. Their beaks are not designed for clearing out holes in trees, and cavities large enough for these big birds to nest may sometimes be hard to find. A pair of toucans may claim a nest hole several weeks before actually laying the clutch of three or four eggs. Like many other birds that live in the Central American forests, keel-billed toucans time their breeding season so that their eggs hatch just before the rainy season begins, late March or early April—even in the rain forest, some months are drier than others. The young toucans grow slowly and appear to leave the nest when they are about seven weeks old. By then, the youngsters are about adult size, but their beaks haven't reached their full size or the full brilliant color of the adults'.

Keel-billed toucan.

CHAPTER TWO

WHAT IS A
RAIN FOREST?

⟨⊶⊶⟩

Rain forests like the one at San Gerardo teem with life that thrives because of the abundant rainfall. A rain forest receives at least 4 inches (20 centimeters) of rain most years during its driest month and usually has far more. Worldwide, tropical rain forests average around 90 inches (230 centimeters) annually. San Gerardo gets several meters of rainfall each year, averaging well over twelve inches a month. As a comparison, the city of Boston, Massachusetts, receives just over 36 inches (about one meter) of rain yearly. The desert city of Yuma, Arizona, gets just under 3.1 inches (8 centimeters) over an entire year.

While there are rain forests in other parts of the world—even in Alaska—the forests with the greatest variety of life are tropical rain forests. Tropical rain forests are found in a wide band spanning the Equator in parts of Asia, Africa, and South and Central America. The yearly seasons so familiar to most North Americans do not exist close to the Equator. The days are always just about twelve hours long, and the temperature varies little from month to month. The temperature in a tropical forest is usually quite warm and never goes below freezing. Some months may be warmer than others, but the difference is nothing like the change from summer to winter in northern latitudes.

Tropical rain forests themselves show a great variety in conditions of temperature and rainfall, depending on their altitude and location. At sea level, the temperature is warmer and more uniform than at higher elevations, where nights may

The rain forest canopy at San Gerardo.

be cool. Rainfall varies, too, both with location and season. While the driest tropical rain forests receive 48 inches (122 centimeters) in a year, the forests on the slopes of Mt. Waialeale in Hawaii can get ten times as much rainfall. Temperature and rainfall variations can have significant effects on forest plants and animals. Around the world, rain forests look quite different from one another and harbor very different assortments of living things.

THE IMPORTANCE OF TROPICAL RAIN FORESTS

In recent years, scientists have become alarmed at the rapid disappearance of tropical rain forests around the world. The forests are being cut down for their wood and burned to make room for crops and cattle pastures.

Why should the destruction of forests in faraway places matter to us? There are many reasons. Many vital medicines have their origins in tropical rain forests, and more remain to be discovered. Scientists and drug companies are hurrying to learn about traditional healing plants from native peoples before the forests where the plants live disappear. Rain forests also yield foods like Brazil nuts and useful substances such as rubber.

Tropical rain forests influence the earth's climate through their cycling of water.

The subject of how forests affect climate is very complicated. But many scientists worry about what will happen to the earth's climate if the rain forests disappear. We know that forests affect local rainfall patterns so that, as the trees are cut down, less rain falls in that area. When forests are burned, huge amounts of carbon are released into the atmosphere, raising CO_2 levels and increasing the "greenhouse effect" that can lead to global warming and drastic changes in climate the world over.

Tropical rain forests such as the Bosque Eterno de los Niños are home to a greater variety of life than any other place on the planet. Whenever a forest is destroyed, these living things lose their homes and are doomed to die. Many of the birds that flash bright colors and sing beautiful songs in our backyards and parks in summertime spend winter in the tropics. Some of these birds are becoming rare, partly because their winter homes are disappearing.

Perhaps the most important reasons for saving the rain forests, however, are difficult to put into words. Whenever humans bring about the destruction of a natural environment, we destroy something that can never be recreated. When a species becomes extinct, it is gone forever. Despite the fact that we live in houses and apartments; wear clothing; get around in cars, buses, and airplanes; and buy our food in supermarkets, we are still a part of nature, and nature is still a part of

Where there is pasture now, forest once stood.

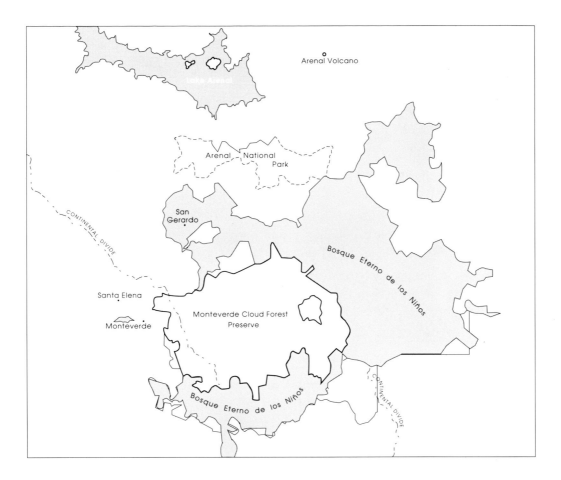

us. The experience of a beautiful spot such as San Gerardo affects a person in ways that cannot be easily expressed, partly because they are so deep and meaningful. For these reasons, every loss of part of the natural world is a loss to humanity as well as to the living things that are directly affected.

HOW FORESTS DIFFER

A tropical rain forest is different from North American forests in many ways. The biggest difference between northern forests and tropical rain forests is the amazing variety of life. No one knows how many species of plants, animals, and other life forms exist in the Children's Rain Forest itself. But it is typical of Costa Rican rain forests, which are especially rich in diversity of living things.

Costa Rica is a small country, about the size of the states of Vermont and New Hampshire combined or the country of Denmark. But it harbors a much greater diversity of species than in the entire United States, which is 180 times its size. Fifteen

These insects called treehoppers are protected from enemies by their resemblance to sharp spines.

This lovely white orchid is an example of tropical forest life.

The strange-looking spiny katydid lives in the Monteverde forests.

This male quetzal breeds only in cloud forests such as Monteverde. (© Michael and Patricia Fogden)

hundred to two thousand kinds of trees grow in Costa Rica, while just 679 are found in the United States. Costa Rica has twice the number of fern species and species of butterflies as the United States, and more than four times as many orchids. Costa Rica has more bird species than in all of North America north of Mexico, including colorful toucans, parrots, and the gorgeous resplendent quetzal. New species of living things are constantly being discovered in Costa Rica. Usually, these are insects like ants or beetles. But recently, a completely new kind of rain forest tree was found near the Bosque Eterno that is not closely related to any others.

Forests in western and northern North America consist mostly of trees like pines and spruce. They have needles that stay on the trees year-round. These trees, called conifers, usually bear branches fairly low on their trunks. Often, most of the trees in the forest are of just one species. In eastern North America, forests are made up mostly of trees like maples, oaks, and hickories. These deciduous trees lose their leaves in the wintertime. The forest has a number of layers. Tall oaks and hickories form the top layer, with the tops of shorter oaks and maples below. Shrubs like dogwood form the lowest aboveground layer, and herbs and mosses clothe the ground.

Rain forest trees reach straight up toward the sky, with few or no branches except near the tops. Each tree produces a thick layer of leafy branches when it reaches the sunlight so that a layer of greenery, called the canopy, blankets the top of the forest. These are called emergent trees. Rain forest trees tend to be tall. The height of the canopy at a place like San Gerardo may be 108 feet (33 meters), with some emergent trees rising several meters higher. Lowland forests have even taller trees, with some emergents stretching to a height of 200 feet or more (60 meters), far above the dense 148-foot (45-meter) high canopy.

No one knows how many different kinds of trees make up a Costa Rican forest such as the Children's Rain Forest, except that there are hundreds. Rain forest trees tend to look similar, and often only an expert can tell the different kinds apart. We also do not know why there is such a variety of species of rain forest trees, or of other living things that live there. Scientists have a number of ideas on the matter, but so far no one can be sure of the reasons.

The undisturbed, mature rain forest canopy is so dense that it keeps most of the sunlight from reaching the forest floor. Most rain forest life is concentrated in the light-rich canopy—that's why a hiker hears many birds but sees few if any. Because there is so little light, few short trees or small plants like bushes or grasses grow in many rain forests, although others have considerable undergrowth. When a tree falls, light streams in and intense new growth begins: shrubs, herbs, small trees, palms, bamboo, and seedlings spring up in the resulting light gap, crowding it with abundant life.

Emergent trees may reach several feet above the canopy, spreading their wide tops above the other trees.

The trees in North American forests usually have deep roots so they can get water even when the weather is dry for a long time. Rain forest trees have shallow roots. Because of the abundant rainfall, the trees can get enough water close to the surface of the ground. Nutrients such as vital minerals are also concentrated near the top in forest soils. Many rain forest trees support themselves with braces, called buttresses, that extend out from the trunks. The nooks and crannies where the buttresses meet the trunk provide homes for small animals from spiders to frogs to bats and snakes.

CLOUD FOREST AND RAIN FOREST

Costa Rica is a mountainous country. Where they haven't been cut, rain forests extend all the way from sea level on the Atlantic side up into the mountains, changing along the way in tree height, rainfall, and other conditions, but still called a rain forest. Atop the mountains, where conditions are right, the forest gradually changes from rain forest into what is called the cloud forest. There is no dividing line between the two forest types. They blend into one another.

A cloud forest like Monteverde differs from a rain forest in a number of ways. Because of the altitude, the temperatures are cooler. Cloud forests are windy places, where moist air from lowland forests sweeps up the slopes. As it reaches the higher altitude, the moisture condenses into a foggy mist that keeps the air moist year-round. Even when there is no rain, the cloud forest stays damp. Cloud forest trees are generally shorter than those in rain forests, probably because of the wind.

Strangler Figs—a Victory in Time

Some of the tallest trees in the rain forest got there literally over other trees. These successful giants are the strangler figs, among the most common trees in the rain forest.

The life of a strangler starts high in the umbrella-like crown of a mature tree, where an abundant harvest of luscious figs awaits. Troops of noisy monkeys and flocks of squawking parrots join with smaller birds in consuming the feast. The tasty fruits contain an abundance of tiny seeds. When one of these seeds passes through the gut of a bird or monkey, it is deposited along with some built-in fertilizer. Where it lands determines if it has a chance of growing into a forest giant itself.

In order for the seed to germinate and grow, its coating must be eaten away by bacteria. This is likely to happen when it lands where there is plenty of organic debris—dead leaves, decaying algae, and so forth, in the crotch of a rain forest tree, where a branch joins the trunk. The germinating seed sends one or more roots downward, toward the forest floor. If a root contacts another bundle of potential nutrients on the way down—perhaps in another crotch—it burrows in and soaks up what it can use. Eventually, the roots reach the ground and penetrate the surface, forming a network of underground roots that will send nutrients to the new shoot growing upward toward the sunlight.

A strangler seedling has a big advantage over seedlings of most forest trees, for it has a headstart on growing into sufficient sunlight. When its leaves reach the canopy, they branch out over those of its host tree, shading the host and slowing its ability to grow and nourish itself. At the same time, the strangler sends down more and more roots, many of which cling to the trunk of the host tree. When two roots touch one another, they join together. Bit by bit, the joining roots encircle the host's trunk and its leaves shade the host tree from above. Eventually, the host tree dies and rots.

While the strangler's life-style may not meet human standards of fairness, it is a boon to other rain forest inhabitants. The nooks and crannies produced by a strangler form homes for everything from tiny insects and spiders to frogs, bats, snakes, and birds. And its fruit feeds many forest animals, sometimes during periods when other food is scarce.

In today's times, when so much of the forest is felled for timber, stranglers are often all that is left. Because they are made up of twisted strands of joined roots and branches, they are good for little but firewood, so loggers leave them standing. Stranglers shade the cattle in many pastures that once were rain forest, while providing homes and food to those forest creatures that can tolerate living away from the protected shade of the forest itself. They are used by birds like parrots and toucans as stopping-off places between forest patches, even when they are not fruiting. For this reason, stranglers have become even more important ecologically than they were before so much of the forests was attacked by axes and chain saws.

A strangler fig winds around the trunk of a tree.

CHAPTER THREE

LIFE IN THE RAIN FOREST

⟨⟩✦✦✦⟨⟩

Studying rain forest life is difficult. Besides the abundant rainfall and often rugged terrain, the small numbers of individuals of many species make scientific work hard. In North America, we are used to visions of vast herds of caribou and meadows awash with color from one kind of wildflower. In the rain forest, the variety of species is great, but the numbers of individuals of any one kind may be very small. At San Gerardo, on a single window I counted twenty-five moths attracted to the lights inside the building, each one a different kind—different color, shape, and size.

Rain forest animals often lead very specialized lives. The colors and patterns on the wings of the moths I saw would hide each one on the bark of a different kind of tree. One species of bee may be adapted to feed on and pollinate only a single species of orchid and may have to fly a mile or more from one flower to the next. An ant species may be found living in just one kind of plant. The incredible variety of life makes each rain forest a very complex system of living things, difficult to study in all its details.

LIVING ON TREES

Many kinds of plants, including orchids, live above the ground in a rain forest or cloud forest, perched on the trunks and branches of the forest giants where the

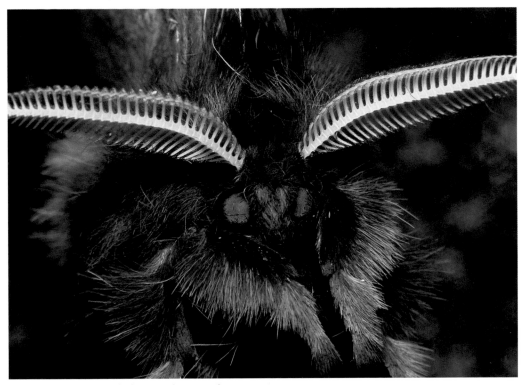

Moths of many kinds live in the rain forest.

light is brighter than at ground level. These plants are called *epiphytes*. They are usually not parasites on the trees and do not take nourishment from the trees. They merely use them for support.

Epiphytes have a number of ways of getting water. Some just dry up when water is scarce and soak it up again when it rains. These plants survive well in a dry condition. Other epiphytes have ways of holding moisture. Some orchids that are epiphytes have special organs that swell up to store water, while plants called tank bromeliads hold water in little pools in their centers. Some epiphytes have thick, leathery leaves that don't dry up easily. Still others send long roots dangling down toward the ground.

The moist cloud forest air nourishes an especially impressive variety of epiphytes. A single cloud forest tree can be host to an incredible number of epiphytes, from mosses and ferns to orchids. Rain and cloud forest tree trunks also support vines rooted in the ground that climb to reach the light. So many vines and epiphytes may grow on a tree that the trunk is almost completely hidden and the branches seem to sprout all sorts of different leaves.

You are probably already familiar with some rain forest plants, although you

Rain and cloud forest tree trunks are often so covered by epiphytes that the trunks themselves can hardly be seen.

This pretty shield-backed bug lives in the Monteverde forest.

don't know it. Most familiar houseplants come from the rain forest. Their ability to survive in reduced sunlight means they can thrive inside a house, and their limited roots can live comfortably in small pots.

RAIN FOREST ANIMALS

The Costa Rican rain forest teems with animal life. Countless kinds of ants clamber over the ground and up and down the tree trunks, while gorgeous butterflies flit through the trees. Beetles, bugs, bees, roaches—all sorts of insects—do well in this warm, moist environment.

Frogs are common rain forest animals. Frogs need to keep their thin skin moist, since they lack the scales of snakes or the thick skin and fur of mammals. The damp forest makes a good home for frogs. The frogs that are familiar to us lay their eggs in ponds in the springtime. But some rain forest frogs never leave the trees. They lay their eggs on leaves or carry them on their bodies, where they develop into tiny frogs before they hatch.

Many cloud forest frogs come out at night.

Rain forest tadpoles often develop in eggs deposited above the water, rather than in the water. When they hatch, the tadpoles drop into the water below. Some develop completely into tiny froglets before even hatching.

The jaguar is the largest predator in the rain forests of Costa Rica.
(© Michael and Patricia Fogden)

The charming coatimundi is a common rain forest mammal.

The striking emerald toucanet is frequently seen in Costa Rican rain forests.

Many mammals live in the Bosque Eterno de los Niños, including six kinds of wild cats. The endangered jaguar is one of them. Jaguars are rare, but raccoon relatives called coatis (co-AH-tees) are common in the forest. They have drawn-out, flexible snouts and long, striped tails held pointing straight upward. Coatis usually travel in groups, wandering about in broad daylight, making curious chittering sounds as they paw through the forest litter looking for food. Other interesting mammals such as tapirs and large rodents called agoutis roam the forest, as well as tiny mice and shrews. Altogether, 209 different kinds of mammals live in Costa Rica, most of them in the rain forests.

Hundreds of bird species make the Children's Rain Forest their home. Flocks of bright green parrots chatter noisily as they fly from treetop to treetop across clearings, while flashy shimmering hummingbirds, some with beaks over an inch long, hover in front of bright red flowers as they feed on nectar. Colorful warblers, some of which travel to the United States to breed in the summer, flit through the trees, and brilliantly colored tanagers frequent the edge of the forest.

WHITE-FACED MONKEYS

White-faced monkeys are commonly seen cavorting in the forest canopy.

The white-faced monkey is one of three kinds that roam the Children's Rain Forest. The other two are spider monkeys and howler monkeys. All three thrive in a variety of habitats, but all need forests for survival. All have *prehensile tails*, tails that can be used like an extra hand or foot for hanging on. The tail may be wrapped around a branch as an anchor while the monkey sleeps or while hanging down to reach tasty morsels of food.

White-faced monkeys are common in Costa Rican forests and live from Belize, north of Costa Rica, southward into northern Colombia in South America. An adult white-faced monkey weighs around 6 pounds (2.7 kilograms). Males tend to be larger than females. These curious creatures live in troops, with usually a dozen or more individuals. Troops of thirty are common. Typically, several males accompany several females, their immature young, and their current nursing babies.

White-faced monkeys are naturally social. From the time an infant is born, other members of the troop want to sniff it and groom its fur. As young monkeys grow up, especially the males, they chase through the branches and have mock battles. Adult males that join the group may also take part in the play.

Female white-faced monkeys give birth to one baby at a time, generally during the drier season. The newborn monkey weighs about a half pound (220 grams). For the first few weeks, the infant hangs onto its mother's fur, riding across her shoulders and then on her back. Bit by bit, the youngster gains independence. At first, it lets go of its mother's fur just for a few moments, but stays right by her side. By the time it is about six months old, the young monkey is big and strong enough to travel on its own, including making jumps of several feet between trees. Even while riding on its mother, the baby reaches out to grab a taste of what its mother eats. In this way, it learns what foods are good to eat. At first, however, its primary source of food is its mother's milk. As it gains independence in other ways, the youngster also depends less and less on milk for nutrition and stops nursing between six months and a year of age.

White-faced monkeys eat a variety of foods, mostly insects and ripe fruits. They begin to feed soon after the sun rises, take a midday break, and resume the hunt for food in late afternoon. They look for food from the forest floor to the tops of the trees. When on the hunt for insects, the monkeys let nothing escape their searching. They tear off dead bark, investigate under leaves, and roll over logs in their hunt for food.

The feeding of these monkeys may benefit some trees. By eating leaves and branches, they increase branching, which might in the long run increase the number of fruits the trees bear. They also remove and eat insect larvae from some kinds of immature fruits, thus preventing destruction of the seeds. Where fruit is abundant, the monkeys may drop large quantitites of fruit to the ground, where it can be reached by ground-dwelling fruit eaters. By eating the fruits of still other trees, the monkeys disperse the seeds and may help them germinate better. In this way, the trees provide food for the monkeys, while the monkeys in turn give trees the service of helping them continue into the next generation.

CHAPTER FOUR

CHILDREN DECIDE TO HELP THE RAIN FOREST

ᏇᏇᏇ

How did children decide to help save the rain forest? The story begins in three different places—Monteverde, Costa Rica; Lewiston, Maine; and a small country school in Sweden. The Costa Rican part of the story actually began in 1949, when Costa Rica abolished its army. In the early 1950s, a small group of people from the United States decided they wanted to live in a peaceful country. These members of the Society of Friends, or Quakers, were morally opposed to war due to the teachings of their religion. They chose Costa Rica as their new home, since it no longer had an army.

After looking at many possible locations, they bought property and established the tiny community of Monteverde, high in the mountains. They purchased land for homes and farms, and they bought the cloud forest that topped the mountains. They decided to leave the forest alone, since their water supply depended on it.

THE THREATENED FOREST

As time went on, the increasing human population of Costa Rica cut down more and more forests to make room for farms. Eventually, Monteverde had one of the few cloud forests left in the country. People realized that this forest was important for plants and animals as well as for the Monteverde water supply. The North American biologists George and Harriet Powell helped the people of Mon-

Forests in Costa Rica and other countries are cut down to make room for farms like this one.

teverde establish the Monteverde Cloud Forest Preserve in 1972. The Quakers turned their portion of the forest over to an organization called the Tropical Science Center to help manage it for the protection of the forest plants and animals.

As the rain forests in the Monteverde area were threatened more and more with destruction, biologists began to understand that the cloud forest could not survive alone. It needed the surrounding rain forests to sustain it. The rain forests help provide the moisture that makes the cloud forest what it is, and many cloud forest animals live part of the time in the rain forest. Some biologists that lived in Monteverde founded the Monteverde Conservation League in 1986. The League was formed to restore deforested areas and conserve them through working with the forest's neighbors, as well as to buy and protect land surrounding the Monteverde Cloud Forest Preserve.

Meanwhile, Sharon Kinsman, a biology teacher at Bates College in Maine, was especially concerned about the plight of Monteverde. She began visiting Monteverde in 1979 and realized what a special place it was. She worried about the destruction around the preserve and developed a slide show and talk about rain forests and why it is important to save them.

This beautiful waterfall at Poco Sol (in the Bosque Eterno de los Niños) has been preserved, thanks to the children of the world.

CHILDREN TO THE RESCUE

During the mid-1980s, in a Swedish country school, teacher Eha Kern and her young students became concerned about the disappearing rain forests around the world. The children kept seeing television programs about interesting animals and beautiful plants. The programs always seemed to end by saying that the plants and animals were disappearing because their homes were being destroyed. The children wished they could find some way to help save the forests.

Eha Kern learned that Sharon Kinsman was spending time in Sweden and asked her to come talk to the children about the Costa Rican rain forest. When Dr. Kinsman finished showing her slides and telling the class about the forest, the children asked, "Can we give some money to save some forest?" Dr. Kinsman suggested helping save the forests around Monteverde. Thus the *Barnens Regnskog* ("Children's Rain Forest" in Swedish) was born.

At first, the children set a goal of raising enough money to buy a small amount of forest, around 25 acres (10 hectares). But through bake sales, presentations of a

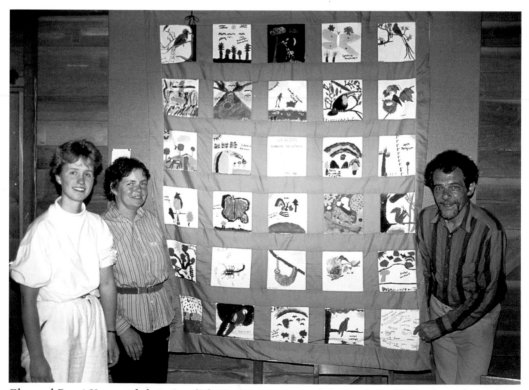

Eha and Berni Kern and their Swedish companion received this quilt as thanks from the children of the Monteverde Friends' School.

COOPERATION IN THE FOREST

Many people see the natural world as a place where living things fight for survival—eat or be eaten. But the relationships between species are often based on cooperation, not competition. Flowering plants would not be able to make the seeds that produce the next generation without the animals that pollinate their blossoms, for example.

In the tropical forest, examples of cooperation abound. One especially interesting type of relationship is between ants and plants. Forest plants compete with one another for a chance at sunlight, and a variety of animals find leaves a good food source. Unlike animals, plants cannot move to get away from their competitors and from those that would eat them—they are rooted in one place. A great variety of plants have developed ways of enticing ants to live in them. The plants provide the ants with homes and often with foods as well. In exchange, the ants attack animals that try to eat the plants and may also remove competing plants, like vines, which threaten their home plants.

A good example of this type of relationship is between *Azteca* ants and the *Cecropia* tree. *Cecropia* is a very common small tree found in rain forests such as El Bosque Eterno de los Niños. Its stem is divided up into a series of hollow segments with walls between. When a young *Azteca* queen is ready to start a new ant colony, she chews her way into a segment of a *Cecropia* stem. She plugs up the hole and stays safely inside while she lays her first batch of eggs and raises her first brood of workers. When those workers come out of their pupas, they chew a hole in the wall of the segment and begin to explore the world outside.

In addition to providing the ants with a home, the *Cecropia* gives them food in the form of small, nutrient-rich lumps of tissue called *Müllerian* bodies. The workers pull out the Müllerian bodies and bring them into the colony segment where they are eaten or stored for future meals.

As the colony grows, it takes over other segments of the stem for raising its ever-growing brood. The workers spend more and more time outside the nest. While the workers are roaming around on the stem and leaves of their home *Cecropia*, they attack insects that are feeding on the plant. Workers from a large colony even stand guard on the undersides of leaves, waiting for invaders. Workers also chew through vines using the *Cecropia* for support. Such vines can become heavy enough to break *Cecropia's* weak branches. A *Cecropia* plant with a resident ant colony looks healthy, with unchewed leaves and a comfortable space around it for growth. One without ants is likely to have ragged leaves and entwining vines climbing its stem.

Both *Cecropia* and *Azteca* have made trade-offs during the establishment of their cooperative relationship. *Azteca* ants have become so specialized that they live nowhere else except inside *Cecropia* stems. If an *Azteca* queen can't find a *Cecropia*, she dies without establishing a colony. The *Cecropia* has to invest some of its energy in producing the Müllerian bodies for the ants to eat. But the trade-offs for both species have been well worth the security against competition and enemies they are able to provide for one another.

Azteca *ants live only inside* Cecropia *trees like this sapling.*

play about the rain forest, and other fund raisers, the children collected more money than they had hoped for. They also arranged for matching money from the Swedish International Development Agency. In only a year's time, they had helped the League out with $100,000. Helping save the forest felt so good they kept on working, and word about their efforts spread around the world.

Sharon Kinsman helped by making arrangements with the Monteverde Conservation League to use the money to buy threatened rain forest. She also founded The Children's Rainforest USA to give American children a way to help. Before long, children's rain forest groups were started in Japan, Germany, and England.

By 1994, about 42,000 acres belonged to the Children's Rain Forest. Most of that land has been saved using dollars, kroner, yen, marks, colones, and all sorts of other money raised with the help and energy of children around the world. And the children haven't quit yet.

CHAPTER FIVE

MANAGING AND USING THE FOREST

⟲〰〰〰⟳

Saving the forest is vital at this time in history, when people with chain saws and axes are working so hard to cut it down. But saving it by buying it is only the first step. The forest must be protected as well. In addition, areas where trees once grew can be returned to forest with the help of people willing to replant, in that way hastening the rebirth of forest.

PATROLLING THE FOREST

What are the threats to the rain forest? The need of poor people to find ways to feed and clothe their families is the greatest threat to rain forests worldwide, not just in Costa Rica. Some rain forest trees are very valuable. A single giant tree of a valuable timber species may be worth thousands of dollars after it is cut down. Without guards to look for illegal loggers, whole areas of the forest can disappear very quickly.

The rain forest harbors other valuable organisms, too. Some animals that live there make good eating and are hunted to put meat on the table. Many beautiful orchids that grow in this moist environment can be sold for good money. Colorful birds also thrive in the forest, birds that people will gladly pay for to keep as "pets." Orchid and bird collectors who prowl the forest can remove a significant amount of the varied life of the forest, upsetting the ecological balance.

Orchids are common rain forest epiphytes, which are removed and sold by poachers.

Settlers, called squatters, also threaten the forest. The land laws in Costa Rica are very complicated and were originally designed to help landless farmers obtain the rights to their own farms and to keep rich landowners from locking up huge plots of land. The most basic law says that if a squatter settles on a piece of land for thirty days without being detected by the landowner, the squatter has some claim to that land. The landowner cannot get rid of him easily. The logic behind this law originally was that if a landowner could not patrol his land in thirty days, he obviously had more land than he needed.

We look at the land differently nowadays than when that law was written. At that time, most people felt that land existed to be developed and used in ways productive to people. But now, so much of the land has gone to human use that we need to protect what wildlands remain. According to the law, however, the protected lands of parks and preserves such as the Bosque Eterno de los Niños are not being "used" in the traditional sense of the word, so they are very much at risk to the squatters.

One solution to the problems of squatters, plant and animal collectors, and

A forest guard patrols the area near San Gerardo in the Bosque Eterno le los Niños.

illegal loggers is forest patrols. The Children's Rain Forest hires teams of forest guards who comb the landscape, looking for intruders. Patrolling the rain forest is hard work, but the guards are dedicated to protecting it. They know their jobs are important. They grew up around the rain forest.

BRINGING BACK THE FOREST

Farmers who live near the Children's Rain Forest are realizing more and more its importance. They have helped replant trees in the regions surrounding the forest —almost a half million trees by the end of 1994. Some of the trees form windbreaks around the farmers' fields, which help keep the hot, dry winds of the Pacific slope from pulling water from their pastures. The farmers have learned that cows in pas-

The Bosque Eterno de los Niños is home to hundreds of species of butterflies and moths.

Costa Rican children help plant trees to renew the forest.

tures with windbreaks yield more milk than in those without. Crop yields improve, too. The more food farmers can produce from their land, the less danger there is that more forest will be cut down. The windbreaks can also supply the farmer with wood needed for fenceposts, firewood, or lumber to build or repair his house so that he does not have to cut down forest trees. In addition, the windbreaks can provide important cover and food for wild animals.

HELPING PEOPLE LEARN

The Monteverde Conservation League believes in the importance of education. When farm families, other Costa Rican citizens, and children learn about the rain forest and cloud forest, they are more likely to want to help preserve them. Caring neighbors can help watch out for squatters and illegal loggers and collectors. Children who grow to love the forest will become adults who want to protect it.

Scientists must also learn about the forest. The rain forest is a complicated place where abundant life thrives and interacts, and we know very little about it. Every year, dozens of new kinds of plants and animals are discovered in the Costa Rican

The research station at San Gerardo, which was still being completed when I visited, is used both for scientific research and for education visits by students and teachers from a number of countries around the world.

rain forest. Scientists work hard to study the forest, but their work has really just begun. The more we understand about how the rain forest works, the better we will be at preserving it. Research stations like the one at San Gerardo provide places where scientists can carry out their studies.

PAYING FOR PROTECTION

All these activities—patrols, tree planting, education, scientific research—take money. Most of the money given to the Children's Rain Forest has been earmarked for land purchase. But the Monteverde Conservation League also needs money to support these other activities. If we are to help the rain forest stay healthy over the decades so that the children of the future can appreciate it, caring for the land is just as important as buying it.

The Monteverde Conservation League is tackling this problem in several ways. They have set up what is called an "endowment fund." The money given to an endowment is not spent. It is invested, and the income from the investments is used for items such as forest guard salaries.

Most of the Children's Rain Forest is set aside for the plants and animals that live there. People are kept out so the forest is not disturbed. But in some carefully chosen areas, the forest is open to travelers, students, and researchers. In these areas, people have a chance to learn about and experience the forest, and the money they spend can be used to help sustain the forest and provide jobs and income for local people.

Conservation groups like the World Wildlife Fund and The Nature Conservancy also help support organizations like the Monteverde Conservation League in their efforts to protect the forest. For example, the World Wildlife Fund and The Nature Conservancy have helped provide funds to buy and protect the San Gerardo area.

Scarab beetles covered with pollen climb over the male flowers on the spadix of an elephant ear. The part of the spadix inside the lower, purple portion of the spathe carries the female flowers. (© Lloyd Goldwasser)

In sunny roadside clearings, pastures, and light gaps in the high Central American forests, where there is plenty of moisture, grows an aptly named plant called "elephant ear." This plant, named by scientists *Xanthosoma robustum*, has a stalk about 4 feet (122 centimeters) tall and a set of up to four leaves over 3 feet (one meter) long and almost as wide.

While its size attracts notice, one of the most interesting things about *Xanthosoma* is its flowers. In North America, most familiar flowers are pollinated by bees, and the seeds of plants are often spread by birds that eat the fruit. In the tropics, life can be much more complicated. While tropical bees and birds are certainly important as pollinators and seed spreaders, other animals take on these roles as well. Elephant ear provides a good example of how these things can happen in the tropics.

Elephant ear is related to some familiar houseplants such as *Philodendron*. You may have seen the flower stalk of such plants—a tall, white or colored bumpy-looking spike, called the *spadix*, backed by a gracefully curved green or white leaflike structure called the *spathe*. *Xanthosoma* has the same sort of flower, only it is 10 inches (24 centimeters) long. While the flower stalk develops, it is protected within the closed spathe. The upper part of the spadix carries male flowers that produce pollen, while the bottom part has the female flowers. Between them, just below a constriction in the spathe, lies a region of sterile flowers that produce neither pollen nor seeds.

When the flowers are ready to bloom, the upper two-thirds or so of the spathe opens, revealing the male flowers. The spadix begins to heat up and releases a sweet scent. As dusk approaches, the heating accelerates until the spadix reaches a temperature between 104° and 107.5° F. (40° to 42° C). The heat intensifies the aroma and helps spread it away from the plant. Within a few minutes, buzzing scarab beetles arrive. They land on the spathe and climb down onto the lower part of the spadix, which is still loosely enclosed by the spathe. The beetles crawl around and eat the sterile flowers. As they move about, pollen on their bodies that they picked up earlier on a different *Xanthosoma* plant gets caught in a sticky orange material on the surface of the female flowers and pollinates them. The beetles stay inside and leave at dusk the next day. At that time, the male flowers release their pollen and heat up to a lesser degree, while the scarabs, covered with pollen, fly off to a new plant.

ELEPHANT EAR AND ASSOCIATES

The relationship between the beetles and elephant ear benefits both. The plant gets its flowers pollinated and the beetles find food. In addition, the chamber at the base of the spadix where they spend the day provides a protected place for the beetles to mate.

If enough of the female flowers are pollinated, the lower part of the stalk stays closed within the spathe while the top part rots and falls off. After the fruit ripens in about two months, the spathe opens and peels back, exposing a coblike knob of about 300 soft green fruits. Bats appear to prefer *Xanthosoma* fruits to many of their other foods. Since bats can fly fast and far, they make good dispersers for the elephant ear's seeds.

Beetles and bats aren't the only creatures that spend time on the *Xanthosoma* flower stalk. Bugs come to suck the juices from the upper part of the spathe and to mate. Flies also show up—one kind appears to eat debris from the spathe, while another lays its eggs on the flowering stalk. Tiny mites hitchhike from one flower stalk to the next on the bodies of the pollinating beetles and drink nectar from the female flowers. Spiders and beetles may come to feed on the great array of insects that inhabit the flower stalk.

Very little is known about the details of the tiny ecosystem that centers about the elephant ear's flower stalk. But, like many interactions of plants and animals in the tropics, it is complex and could reveal many more interesting facts with further study.

Elephant ears are among the easiest plants to recognize in the rain forest.

CHAPTER SIX

PEOPLE TOGETHER WITH THE FOREST

When I arrived at the outpost of San Gerardo in the Bosque Eterno de los Niños, the first people I met had come from England—two teachers, two boys, and two girls. They had traveled halfway around the world to help build a research station in the forest clearing and to see the land they helped to save. When they got to the station, all the rooms were open to the forest air. But in a few short days, they helped install the doors and windows, making the place more comfortable for the visitors who would follow them, like me.

This group had a special love for the Bosque Eterno. For several years, the children of their South Craven School in Yorkshire held bake sales and auctions. They worked hard cleaning a polluted stream in exchange for contributions from local businesses and planted trees to earn money from sponsors. With these and other activities, the school raised more than $7,000 for the Children's Rain Forest. Now the representatives of the school were on their way home, excited about sharing their adventure with those who sponsored their trip and with nature groups. Visiting the forest and helping build the station made them even more eager to continue to raise money for the forest.

THE SAN GERARDO EXPERIMENT

The rain forest can only survive if people can also find ways of making a living while keeping the forest intact. The people of the small settlement at San Gerardo are working hard to learn how to share the land with nature. Jobs at the research station help the people support their families. An organic garden at the forest edge grows food both for families and for station guests. The residents spend a great deal of time meeting together to plan ways to improve their lives while working to help keep the forest healthy.

Visitors to San Gerardo share in the work. Members of our group built dining tables and cleared hiking trails. A student and I spent a morning helping to plant onions, tomatoes, and peas that would feed future visitors to the station while Máximo, the gardener, told us of his love for the forest animals. We helped harvest the beans that later showed up on the dinner table. As we worked, we listened to birds calling from the trees and felt the gentle, warm rain on our backs. Working in that garden with Máximo and surrounded by the beauty of the forest made me feel deep inside just how important it is to preserve the natural world and to learn to share the earth with other living things. Knowing that the children of the world are willing to help in these difficult tasks makes me optimistic that the children of the future will be able to experience the wildness and wonder of the forest as I have done.

Volunteers from the South Craven School in Yorkshire, England, helped put the finishing touches on the research station at San Gerardo.

Heliconia plants are common throughout the rain forests of Costa Rica.

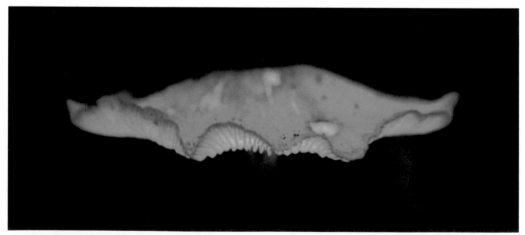

The forests of Costa Rica are full of surprises like this phosphorescent mushroom.

Bromeliads—Living Successfully Aboveground

Among the many epiphytes in the rain forest, the dozens of species of tank bromeliads are among the most successful. These graceful plants have developed their own built-in, water-storage system. Bromeliads have no long stem from which leaves grow. Instead, the leaves all originate at the bottom of the plant and arch outward and upward. The bases of the leaves are wide and overlap generously. At the bottom, they press tightly against one another, but higher up, they are curved outward. Rain falling on the leaves is channeled along the curves of the leaves downward to the center of the plant, where it gathers in a pool. The tank size of a full-grown bromeliad varies tremendously, from less than a teaspoon to about 5.5 gallons (20 liters).

Bromeliads produce beautiful flower stalks.

As long as rainfall is sufficient, the storage tank at its center provides enough water for a tank bromeliad, and its perch on a tree gives it access to light. But a plant needs more than water and light; it also requires minerals. Soil-rooted plants absorb minerals from the soil. But an epiphyte does not have access to soil minerals, so it needs to get them in another way. When rain falls on the forest canopy, some minerals become leached from leaves of plants higher up and dissolved in the rain before it reaches a bromeliad. Dead leaves and dust particles can also be trapped within the tank, providing some minerals.

Probably the greatest source of minerals for a tank bromeliad is the wealth of living things that take up residence in such an airborne pool. While even a large bromeliad tank may be small as pools go, it offers some advantages for small forms of life. For one, few predators are likely to search for food in these tucked-away places. And few competitors for food and space are likely to share the tank either. One scientist found 342 different species of animals living in bromeliad tanks, and many more have been found since his studies. The water-soluble wastes of all this life provide a convenient source of nitrogen and other minerals to the bromeliad.

What kinds of living things can make a life in such a small body of water? A variety of protozoans, which are microscopic, single-celled creatures able to dry up and blow from place to place on the wind, make tanks their homes. Small, freshwater animals adapted to life in short-lived pools can also live in tanks, some feeding on the protozoa. Worms, snails, and beetles are among tank inhabitants. A number of mosquito species lay their eggs in tanks, where their larvae can develop away from the fish that would eat them in ponds. Perhaps the most interesting tank residents, however, are tadpoles. Some colorful frogs that spend their adult lives on the forest floor actually climb into the trees to lay their eggs or deposit tadpoles in bromeliad tanks. The female frog of one kind backs down and lays a single egg in the pool of one plant, then finds other bromeliads as homes for the rest of her eggs. As the tadpoles grow, she returns to their tiny pools and lays unfertilized eggs that would never hatch in the tanks. These eggs serve as food for the tadpoles. Other kinds of frogs live as adults in bromeliad tanks, where the miniature forest of surrounding leaves helps protect them from predators. The tank of each individual bromeliad is thus a tiny ecosystem of its own, home to a variety of life that has adapted to this unique environment.

THE CHILDREN'S RAIN FOREST AND YOU

⟨⟩✦✦✦⟨⟩

VISITING THE CHILDREN'S RAIN FOREST

If you are lucky enough to be able to travel to Costa Rica, you can visit part of the Children's Rain Forest as well as Monteverde Cloud Forest Preserve. Nature trails in the Monteverde area run through the Bajo del Tigre area of the Children's Rain Forest, where swallow-tailed kites soar on the breeze and bellbirds make their unique "bonk" sounds from the treetops.

Ecological workshops are offered at San Gerardo and another part of the Children's Rain Forest, Poco Sol, for teachers and high school students that focus on environmental education, natural history, and sustainable development. Plans are in place for an education center to be built. Interested groups should contact the Monteverde Conservation League for more information.

WHAT YOU CAN DO

Around the world, children are raising money, all with the goal of helping preserve this beautiful forest. Helping the Bosque Eterno is not difficult. All it takes is a good idea and plenty of hard work. Classroom groups, scout troups, church groups, conservation clubs, and individual children—all have pitched in.

Money can be raised in a number of ways besides bake sales and car washes.

The South Craven School children held auctions. Children brought in toys and other things they no longer wanted that were bought by children who did want them. They also held raffles, a stream cleanup, and tree plantings. For one raffle, British TV personality and bird-watcher Bill Oddie donated an original painting.

Individuals as well as groups can gather contributions. Twins in California invited friends to a birthday party that included a visit to a local zoo and asked for donations to the Children's Rain Forest instead of gifts. Other children have requested donations instead of Christmas gifts from their families.

The children in some classrooms have created their own indoor rain forests and charged schoolmates, families, and friends to visit them, then given the proceeds to the Children's Rain Forest. One class saved two thousand pennies, then wrote a check at the end of the year.

Rain forest greeting cards are available at low cost from Dan Perlman for groups interested in helping nature preserves. A portion of the proceeds he receives goes directly to the Bosque Eterno, and those selling the cards can also contribute their profits. Contact Dan Perlman, P. O. Box 610323, Newton, MA 02161-0323.

Projects directly related to conservation, such as a recycling campaign, are especially good ways to raise money. Carrying out a cleanup project for a local stream or vacant lot, with people sponsoring the children to work by the hour, is another constructive idea.

Contributions to the Bosque Eterno de los Niños can be made in a number of ways. The most direct is through the Monteverde Conservation League, Apartado 10581-1000, San Jose, Costa Rica, Central America. When you contribute directly to the League, you can let them decide how best to use your contributions, or you can specify that they be used for environmental education, building the education center, forest patrols, land purchase, or another use. Contributions can also be made by way of The Nature Conservancy, International Children's Rain Forest Program, 1815 North Lynn Street, Arlington, VA 22209 (specify that you want the money to go to the Monteverde Conservation League); The Children's Rainforest, P. O. Box 936, Lewiston, ME 04240; World Wildlife Fund, 90 Eglinton Avenue E., Suite 501, Toronto, Ontario, M4P 2Z7, Canada; or Children's Tropical Forests U.K., 8 Midgate, Peterborough PE1 1TN, England. Japan and Sweden also have their own organizations.

GLOSSARY

Bosque Eterno de los Niños The Spanish name for the International Children's Rain Forest

Bromeliad A kind of plant with leaves growing from the base that form a water-holding tank.

Buttresses Extensions from the trunk of a tree that help support it.

Canopy The thick layer of branches of leaves atop the forest.

Cloud forest A mountaintop forest which is usually enveloped in clouds so that the leaves of the plants are nearly always wet.

Deciduous tree A tree that loses its leaves before winter or before the dry season.

Emergent tree A tree that extends above the forest canopy.

Epiphyte A plant that attaches itself to another plant rather than being rooted in the soil.

Greenhouse effect The accumulation of carbon dioxide in the atmosphere that results in global warming.

Light gap A sunlit area in the forest brought about by the falling of a tree.

Monteverde Conservation League The conservation organization that administers the Children's Rain Forest.

Müllerian bodies Growths on the *Cecropia* plant that ants feed on.

Rain forest A forest defined as one that receives at least four inches of rain each month of the year. Most rain forests receive much more moisture.

Spadix The spike-shaped flower stalk of plants like the elephant ear or *Philodendron*

Spathe The curved leaflike structure that envelopes the developing spadix.

INDEX